MORE REFLECTIONS

Hope in Times of Adversity

Logo by de'Zengo Designs

DORIS HAVER ROUSE

Copyright © 1994, **Doris Haver Rouse**
Library of Congress, Washington D.C. USA
Printed in the United States

All rights reserved. No part of this publication may be reproduced, distributed or transmitted in any form or by any means, without prior written permission of the author as permitted in accordance with Title 17, United States Code.

Scripture taken from the "New King James Version" Copyright © 1982 by Thomas Nelson, Inc. Used by permission. All rights reserved.
Printed in the United States

Book Layout © 2014 BookDesignTemplates.com
Cover Photo © 2014 Chip Rouse
Editing: Content Visionary; Diona Reeves

More Reflections, Doris Haver Rouse-1st ed.
ISBN-13: 978-1499164947
ISBN 10: 1499164947

Foreword

It has been said, "Pain is inevitable; misery is optional." Nothing is more important in times of suffering in the life of a Christian than choosing faith, hope and trust over misery and despair. This involves recognizing our pain and identifying our fears in an attitude of trust in God's promise to 'work in all things for our good and His purposes." (Romans 8:28)

We spend so much time and energy trying to please or appease God when what He really wants is to connect with us and help us to grow in our knowledge of Him through a personal relationship with Him through Jesus Christ. So often the greatest opportunity for spiritual growth comes during times of adversity when we face our powerlessness and trust His sovereign power to do for us what we cannot do for ourselves. Losses, which are inevitable in life, then become gains as the loss of earthly comforts open the door for us to experience divine comfort, and God becomes more real to us than ever before.

More Reflections is a collection of poems written during a time of adversity where the reality of God's loving presence and power overshadowed the pain and loss I was experiencing. It was my way of expressing newfound understandings of God's truths as revealed through His Word and seeking to grow in my own knowledge and understanding of Him. Taken from daily journals and times of prayer and meditation, I share them with the hope of encouraging others to find their own unique ways of communicating with God through prayer and seeking to relate to Him on a personal level.

                    Doris Haver Rouse

Dedication

Everyone needs a cheerleader! I have been blessed with many in the course of my career and 'growing up' years and see each one as a gift from God to encourage me in my faith and inspire me to seek His best for my life. In addition to my family, I am grateful for a very special friend who has encouraged me personally as well as cheered me on in my writing ministry.

One of my staunchest writing cheerleaders is a former member of a youth group of which I was the leader at what is now the First Baptist Church of Fairview Heights, Illinois. (Newly married and a recent college graduate, I was not much older than the youth I was charged with leading.) Among the youngest members was a preteen who some years later became a close friend and a great source of encouragement as well as an example of facing adversity with a godly perspective.

Not a stranger to adversity herself, I have watched her emerge from life's painful realities with a deeper faith and compassionate, caring concern for others—a positive outcome of adversity. She has always enthusiastically supported me – to even promoting my books in various outlets. I am indebted to you, *Margie McDaniel Miller,* not only for your friendship and support but your inspiring witness over the years. May God continue to bless you and your husband, Guy, as you continue to minister to others in loving, encouraging and joy-filled ways.

To that special friend of all friends, our Lord Jesus Christ, who is *always* ready to cheer us on, I offer the utmost praise. It is with deep gratitude that I seek to serve Him with that with which I have been gifted. To Him be all the honor and glory and praise!

Doris Haver Rouse

Contents

Foreword
Dedication

Focus	1
Beyond the Pain	2
Purification	3
God is Love	5
Obedience	6
Harmony	7
Spider Webs	9
Answered Prayer	10
Harmony	11
God's Silences	13
Comfort	14
Teach Us	15
Pitfalls	17
Submission	18
Our Calling	19
Refuge	21
Crossroads	22
Faith	23
Clarity	25
Uncertainties	26
The Listener	27
Walls	28
I Believe	29
Promise	30

Abiding Love	31
Anticipation	33
Salvation	34
Transformation	35
Little Things	37
Perspective	38
Certainty	39
Security	41
Because	42
Perseverance	43
Fog/Trust	45
Assurance	46
Intimate moments	47
Nighttime Prayer	49
Reminders	50
Heavenly Account	51
Credits	52

*"Keep your heart with all diligence,
for out of it spring the issues of life."
Proverbs 4:23*

"

*"But seek first the kingdom of God and His righteousness,
and all these things shall be added to you."*
Mathew 6:33

Focus

In times of pain and sorrow,
Or when troubles plague our soul,
Is the time to focus upward
To the One who's in control.

And by faith, trust He is present
With His ever-watchful eye;
Believing He will listen,
And will hear each heartfelt cry.

For as we wait upon Him,
Fix our thoughts on heaven above,
Our darkness turns to sunshine
Through the power of His love.

"Is any among you suffering? Let Him pray."
James 5:13

Beyond the Pain

Beyond the pain is peace and joy,
Beyond the darkness, light;
If we but trust the Father's love,
Walk by faith and not by sight.

Beyond the pain is mercy, grace,
Hope forevermore;
If, as the Spirit gently knocks,
We open our heart's door.

Beyond the pain is strength and life,
Such as we've never known.
For as we turn to Him in faith,
He brings comfort to His own.

"God, who knows the heart, acknowledged them by giving them the Holy Spirit...purifying their hearts by faith."
Acts 15:8-9

Purification

Hold on to me, Lord,
As the flames grow hotter, higher.
Hold on to me, Lord,
As You purify me by Your fire,
And bring me out in deeper faith,
With greater joy in what I do,
By burning those impurities
That hinder my following You.

Hold on to me, Lord,
As the pain grows in intensity.
Hold on to me, Lord,
Until I am restored in purity,
And by Your staying power and grace,
Deliver me in such a way
That I will witness to the love
That comes from You today.

"God is love."
"1 John 4:2

God is Love

God is love…
In a world where hatred abounds.
God is love…
In Him new life is found.
God is love…
And as trials come our way,
We can trust in His divine control
As we yield to His will and pray.
God is love…
What a glorious, encouraging thought.
God is love…
The crucial battle has been fought.
God is love…
And through the cross of Calvary,
God's love and grace are ours to claim,
As by His power we are set free!
God is love…
All created life proclaims.
God is love…
We are transformed by His name.
God is love…
His Spirit gently bids us come,
Receive the love He freely gives
Through the atonement of His Son.

…"to obey is better than sacrifice."
1 Samuel 15:22

Obedience

Moment by moment obedience,
Abandoned to His will and plan.
Focusing steadfastly on Him,
Despite trials and turmoil at hand.

Remaining faithful and true to His nature,
From all doubt and self-pity refrain.
This is God's will for His children,
How we honor and glorify His name.

Reaching out to the oppressed and discouraged,
Offering cups of water in His loving name.
When sharing the burdens of others,
We give witness to the love that we claim.

"…this is the victory that has overcome the world….our faith."
1 John 5:4

Inner Victory

Sometimes our lives are altered
By the pain that comes our way,
And we struggle to find strength to stand,
To overcome and pray.

As we kneel before the Father,
Through the Cross of Christ, the Son,
And we listen to His quiet voice,
The battle then is won.

Then we arise and walk victoriously,
Believing He is near,
And the love that only He can give,
Drives out our doubt and fear.

So in times of pain and sorrow,
If we are still and seek His voice,
We'll discover He is with us,
And find reason to rejoice.

"He who has begun a good work in you will complete it until the day of Jesus Christ."
Philippians 1:6

Spider Webs

Spider webs remind me, Lord,
Of Your mysterious ways;
This masterpiece conceived at night
Brings wonder to my days.

Each delicate and silky thread
So carefully is spun,
To complete the overall design,
For which it was begun.

Just as each deed or action
Is woven by Your hand,
Every circumstance, though simple,
Supports Your master plan.

"So I say to you, ask and it will be given you; seek and you will find; knock, and it will be opened to you."
Luke 11:9

Answered Prayer

O' Lord,
I prayed a simple prayer in faith,
Believing in Your word.
But when the answer did not come,
I wondered if You'd heard.

And then one day in sheer delight,
A spontaneous surprise.
I saw the answer to my prayers
Revealed before my eyes.

And so I've learned to pray and wait,
To watch expectantly,
For answers to each heartfelt prayer,
As I wait patiently.

"My grace is sufficient for you...."
2 Corinthians 12:9

Harmony

Like sunshine and rain,
Both pleasure and pain
Play a role in our lives day by day.
And while neither alone
Will be solely our own,
We find both will accompany our way.

And so we must heed
In both our want and our need,
To look to the Father above;
To grant us His power,
And sustain us each hour,
By His marvelous grace and deep love.

*"Now faith is the substance of things hoped for,
the evidence of things not seen."*
Hebrews 11:1

God's Silences

God's silences remind us
Of our dependent, helpless ways,
Of our inability to control
Events that sometimes plague our days.

For in times of pain and sorrow
When it appears He is not there,
We must trust with mind and heart and soul
That He is present and He cares.

For as we look to Him in faith,
Persevere and overcome;
We discover with delight, surprise,
A new victory has been won.

*"Blessed be the God and Father of our Lord Jesus Christ…
who comforts us in all our tribulation….."
2 Corinthians 1:3*

Comfort

In times of illness or sorrow,
Keep us ever mindful, Lord,
That You are always present
As You've promised in Your Word.

And no matter what we suffer
From our pain or tragic loss,
Nothing can compare to that
Which You suffered on the Cross.

So grant us grace to see beyond
Our pain to heaven's shore,
Where one day in Your Presence
We'll experience pain no more.

*"I have set before you life and death…
therefore, choose life...."*
Deuteronomy 30:19

Teach Us

Lord, teach us how to live
In the valley day by day,
Focused on Your kingdom's work,
Submissive to Your way.

Teach us how to listen, Lord,
To hear Your Spirit's voice,
And despite the darkness of the hour,
Find reason to rejoice.

Teach us, Lord, discernment,
That Your gentle voice we'll heed;
Then follow in faith and obedience,
In *whatever* way You lead.

"You shall have no other gods before me."
Exodus 20:3

Pitfalls

When life turns from sunny,
Bright days into rain,
So oft' we are tempted
To look in our pain —
To other resources
Though short-lived they be,
For solace and comfort,
From our pain to be free.

But true hope and real comfort
Are not to be found
In those earthly enticements
That we find all around;
But only as we
Seek our refuge in Him,
Will we discover His peace
And new joy from within.

"Come to Me, all you who labor and are heavy laden, and I will give you rest."
Matthew 11:28

Submission

How difficult it is, Lord,
To come by faith submissively;
As a child comes to his father,
In childlike trust, simplicity.

Yet only in our coming,
As our hearts we humbly yield,
Will we receive Your wondrous grace
By Your love be truly healed.

So draw us closer to You, Lord,
Keep us dependent day by day;
By Your Spirit make us a witness to
Your highest will and way.

*"If you abide in My word,
you are My disciples indeed."*
John 8:31

Our Calling

God did not call us to earthly success,
Nor to material wealth or gain,
But rather to be instruments
Of the righteousness we gain.

He did not equip us for victory
As earthly standards go,
But rather to be stewards
Of the gifts on us He bestows.

He gave His life that we might have
Abundant life so free,
And in return we yield our lives
That others, too, may see.

"God is our refuge and strength; a very present help in trouble. Therefore we will not fear, though the earth be removed and the mountains be carried into the midst of the sea."
Psalm 46:1-2

Refuge

Help us, Lord,
In the midst of pain and loss
To not give in to dread, despair,
But focus on the Cross.

For on the Cross of Calvary,
Victory over death was won,
Freeing us from fear and doubt,
Through Jesus Christ, Your Son.

Help us, Lord,
Overcome our fearful ways,
And walk by faith in light and love,
Giving You all glory and praise.

*"I delight to do your will, O my God,
and Your law is within my heart."*
Psalm 40:8

Crossroads

I came to the crossroads
And knew not which way to go.
I could not see beyond the bend,
If I'd find friend or foe.

I paused in prayer, submissively,
In moments quiet and still,
And sought with all my heart and soul,
To discern the Father's will.

I heard His gentle voice so soft,
His Spirit led the way;
As I stepped out in faith and trust,
I new He'd lead the way.

"The just shall live by faith..."
Romans 1:17

Faith

I asked, dear Lord,
That You might lead
That I might see Your way;
I sought to know Your will and plan
In all my steps today.
The answer to my cry for help
Came quietly, yet clear;
I knew it was the truth, the way,
I felt Your Presence near.
The way to follow is recorded
In Your written plan;
"The just shall live by faith" it says,
The need of every man.
I come in need of greater faith
To be all You desire I be;
For only by Your Spirit's power
Is Your life made real in me.
I ask for strength and faith, dear Lord,
Detachment from above,
That I may face life's realities,
In joy and peace and love.

"For we walk by faith, not by sight."
2 Corinthians 5:7

Clarity

Slowly moving into the fog
The way ahead unclear;
The tugboat inches on its course,
Trusting light will soon be near.

Ever moving forward by faith,
Unsure of obstacles ahead,
Certain the fog will disappear,
Bringing clarity instead.

Thus, our journey sometimes is hindered,
By fog that confuses, impedes;
But if we, by faith, move into its midst,
We discover the light that we need.

*"Jesus Christ is the same
yesterday, today and forever."*
Hebrews 13:6

Uncertainties

O' Lord,
When faced with life's uncertainties
Grant us faith to trust You are near.
And despite the unknown that awaits us,
Not give in to doubt and fear.

For our hope is not in circumstance,
In the good or evil done;
But in the Cross of Calvary
Where the victory over death was won.

So grant us grace to walk in peace,
In strength down life's path trod,
With assurance You are in control,
Because You, alone, are God.

"He is also able to save to the uttermost those who come to God through Him, since He always lives to make intercession for them."
Hebrews 7:25

The Listener

Listening can be loving
As we walk life's paths today;
If we but intercede that all
Might know the Father's way.

For He alone is able
To direct the path we trod;
For no one sees as He sees,
Our loving Father, God.

And so when others come to us
And their burdens they seek to share;
Our response in love is listening,
Interceding for the Father's care.

For He alone sees everything,
He alone knows best;
And He and only He can give
Sweet peace and inner rest.

"Forgive and you will be forgiven."
Luke 6:37b

Walls

Brick by brick,
One unresolved hurt after another,
Resentment on top of resentment,
The wall gets higher and thicker;
And the love that was once alive
Grows cold and dies.
Brick by brick,
One kind act after another,
Forgiveness on top of forgiveness,
The wall crumbles,
Creating an opening;
And the love that once appeared dead
Is energized and thrives.

"Without faith it is impossible to please Him, for he who comes to God must believe that He is, and that He is a rewarder of those who diligently seek Him."
Hebrews 11:6

I Believe

I believe, Lord;
Help thou mine unbelief,
As I bring this burden to You,
Seek Your comfort, hope, relief.

I believe, Lord;
Grant me power from within,
To walk by faith triumphantly
In victory over sin.

"I will never leave you nor forsake you."
Hebrews 13:5

Promise

"I will never leave you nor forsake you."
Your faithful promise doth remain,
And as I come to You by faith,
Your strength and power are mine to claim.

And so in simple trust I come,
Place my life into Your hands,
And wait submissively in faith,
As You fulfill Your plan.

*"If we love one another, God abides in us, and
His love has been perfected in us."*
1 John 4:12

Abiding Love

Lord, thank You for assurance
Of Your love and grace each day;
For the knowledge I am loved, secure,
WHATEVER comes my way.

Thank You for that Spirit, Lord,
That guides me day by day,
And keeps me mindful of Your love,
Your light and truth and way.

Lord, thank You, for Your promised Word,
To be faithful and with me remain;
For strength to face life's troubles and trials
As Your power and grace I claim.

Photo by Chip Rouse © 2014

"Look at the birds of the air, for they neither sow nor reap nor gather into barns; yet your heavenly Father feeds them. Are you not of more value than they."
Matthew 6:26

Anticipation

I saw a bluebird fluttering about
One cold and wintry day,
And thought with hope and comfort,
"Spring must not be far away."
I felt a sense of gratitude
For this simple sign of cheer
That the dreary days of winter
Would eventually disappear.
And I remembered days of trial
When life was difficult to bear,
But after patiently enduring them,
Discovered God was always there.
And I felt a sense of triumph
As I reflected on those days;
When evil seemed so in control,
And there seemed little cause for praise.
So as I face these changes
That bring joy and sorrow, too;
I'm assured of God's own Presence,
And His strength to see me through.
For one day there'll be no winter,
Pain and suffering will be no more;
What a glorious celebration
Will be ours 'yon heaven's shore.

"For God did not send His Son into the world to condemn the world, but that the world through Him might be saved."
John 3:17

Salvation

God looked down from heaven
Sought man's worship and his praise,
But saw instead his evil deeds,
His rebellious, sinful ways.

And so in mercy and in love,
Devised a special plan;
He chose to send His only Son
As sacrifice for man.

Some believed and followed,
While others turned away;
But God, the Father, through the Son
Still offers grace today.

"Do not be conformed to this world, but be transformed by the renewing of your mind that you may prove what is that good and acceptable and perfect will of God."
Romans 12:2

Transformation

I feel Your loving presence, Lord,
Sense Your healing power near;
Find peace and joy and calmness
As Your love drives out all fear.

I bow in worship and gratitude,
My heart overflows in praise;
As I ponder Your great love for me,
See Your hand in all my days.

And as I come to You by faith,
Yield to You my heart and soul;
I discover Your transforming power,
As You cleanse and make me whole.

"Assuredly, I say to you, inasmuch as you did it to one of the least of these My brethren, you did it to Me."
Matthew 25:40

Little Things

It's the little things that count, Lord,
That seem to make our day;
A smile, a hug, a handshake,
Another's prayer along the way.

A gift of summer's produce,
An encouraging note of cheer;
All little gifts that lift our hearts,
And remind us You are near.

It's the little things that count, Lord,
That bring heaven's love to earth;
A visit to a shut-in,
The rejoicing in a birth.

A pot of stew, a pan of rolls,
A helping hand for one who ails;
All little things that witness to
Your love that never fails.

"Be diligent to present yourself approved to God, a worker who does not need to be ashamed, rightly dividing the word of truth."
2 Timothy 2:15

Perspective

We think we have the answers,
That we truly know our God;
And then difficulties come our way,
As life's troubled path we trod.

And we realize with humility
And stark reality,
That our God is so much greater
Than the tiny view we see.

And so we seek to understand,
To in our knowledge grow;
Of that One whom we will never fully
Understand and know.

And in our searching and seeking,
As we discover day by day;
We grow in oneness with Him
And more clearly see His way.

"There is no fear in love…"
1 John 4:18 a

Certainty

Lord,
I know not what lies before me,
But I trust that You are near;
And the knowledge of Your Presence
Drives out all my doubt and fear.

For I know that You will guide me
By Your loving, gracious hand;
As You've guided other pilgrims
To that blessed Promised Land.

And so I wait and pray and trust
Until the way is clear;
And then step out in faith because
You've canceled all my fear.

"For I am persuaded that neither death nor life, nor angels nor principalities nor powers, nor things present nor things to come, nor height nor depth, nor any other created thing, shall be able to separate us from the love of God which is in Christ Jesus our Lord."
Romans 8:38-39

Security

It suddenly appeared from nowhere
On a snowy, wintry day;
The sun appearing through the clouds,
Bringing light to a gloomy day.

And so God's loving Spirit comes,
Suddenly, by surprise;
Bringing hope and reassurance,
Promise of His counsel wise.

And somehow my days so troubled,
Are less burdened, for I see
That nothing that's external
Can separate God's love from me."

*"For the death that He died, He died to sin once for all,
but the life that He lives, He lives for God."*
Romans 6:10

Because

Because He trusted the Father,
We walk in faith and not in fear.
Because His love is unconditional,
We can feel His presence near.

Because He suffered for our sins
With pain we cannot comprehend,
We can go to Him for comfort
And know He understands.

Because He loves each sinner,
While hating evil and all sin,
We can intercede and trust that He
Will transform hearts from within.

"Pray without ceasing."
1 Thessalonians 5:17

Perseverance

Grant us grace to wait, Lord,
Your sacred word to heed;
To trust that You have heard our cry
And You know our every need.

Teach us perseverance, Lord,
Based on hope and not on fear;
That we may see Your power at work
As we trust Your Presence near.

Draw us to Your love, O Lord,
Comfort, fill our soul;
Strengthen as we wait on You,
Finding joy in Your control.

Grant us patience to wait, Lord,
Believing You will come;
Grace to watch and pray in faith,
Until the victory is won.

*"Trust in the Lord and do good;
dwell in the land and feed on His faithfulness."
Psalm 37:3*

Fog

Fog has settled over the earth, Lord,
Obscuring my view;
Cloaking trees and branches
In a smoke-like film.
While I know that beyond the fog is visibility,
For the present I must trust that which I cannot see;
And move forward by faith,
Knowing that "this too shall pass",
And when the fog lifts, there will be clarity and light.

Trust

To trust You in the midst of pain
To walk by faith each day
Involves continually letting go,
Submitting to Your way.
To trust You when the way is dim,
The path ahead obscure;
Requires a steadfast spirit that
Is trusting and secure.
And so I come to You, dear Lord,
I seek Your Spirit's lead;
For grace to walk in truth and light,
Sufficient for each need.

*"Trust in the Lord with all your heart,
And lean not on your own understanding;
In all your ways acknowledge Him,
And He shall direct Your paths."*
Proverbs 3:5-6

Assurance

I trust You, Lord,
Although I may not understand
The reason for the suffering
That comes to me through Your hand.

I trust You, Lord,
Though I cannot always see,
How You will work for good and use
Each trial and adversity.

I trust You, Lord,
With my mind and heart and might,
And claim Your promised power and grace
As I walk by faith, not sight.

"There is no fear in love; but perfect love casts out fear."
1 John 4:18

Intimate Moments

O' Lord,
How desperately we seek to flee
From circumstances painful and grim,
Failing to see the opportunity
That Your Spirit offers within.

For in those times of deepest pain
Those moments of doubt and despair;
Your Spirit draws us to Your breast,
You deepest love to share.

And as we bring our sorrow, our pain,
By faith and trust, believe;
Your perfect love drives out our fears,
As Your peace and hope we receive.

*"Evening and morning and at noon I will pray and cry aloud,
And He shall hear my voice."
Psalm 55:17*

Nighttime Prayer

As day is drawing to a close,
I bow my head in prayer, dear Lord;
And thank You for Your love and grace,
The truths found in Your Word.

I thank You for Your faithfulness,
Your comfort, sweet release;
For deliverance from temptation's snare,
For abiding joy and peace.

I ask for grace for those dear Lord,
I lift in prayer to You;
And pray that You will bless each soul,
As only You can do.

"Be anxious for nothing, but in everything by prayer and supplication, with thanksgiving, let your requests be made known to God; and the peace of God, which surpasses all understanding will guard your hearts and minds through Christ Jesus."
Philippians 4: 6-7

Reminders

Sunrises and sunsets,
Events I daily see;
That remind me of Your faithfulness,
Of Your love and care for me.

Unbidden, not beckoned,
Gracious gifts of love and grace;
Evidence of Your holy Presence, Lord,
Everywhere in every place.

While I may not always notice
Each day they reappear;
Heaven-sent reminders,
Or Your love that's always near.

*"Grace to You from God, our Father
and the Lord Jesus Christ."
1 Thessalonians 1:1*

Heavenly Account

God's love and grace and mercy
Are like a bank account each day;
That I must draw upon by faith
As I seek His will and way.

For through the giving of Himself,
Jesus Christ prepared the way;
For me to come by faith in Him,
Receive His love and grace today.

For by His death, my legacy
Was deposited and sealed;
And through each day's withdrawal,
His precious treasures are revealed.

Credits

A special thank you to the following contributors:

Diona Reeves: Content Visionary; Editing/Design
Chip Rouse: Cover photo and bluebird photo
De'Zengo Designs: Reflections Logo

For additional information regarding
other books in this series, see:

Facebook: Reflections
Or contact the author at:
www.prayerandrefletions.com
prayerandreflections@yahoo.com

Made in the USA
Middletown, DE
01 September 2015